Math = Fun!™

Multiplication
and
Division

by Jerry Pallotta
Illustrated by Rob Bolster

SCHOLASTIC INC.

New York   Toronto   London   Auckland   Sydney
Mexico City   New Delhi   Hong Kong   Buenos Aires

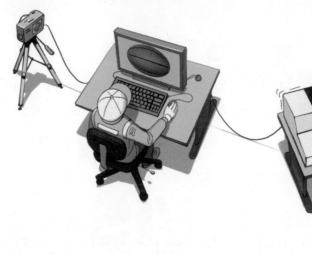

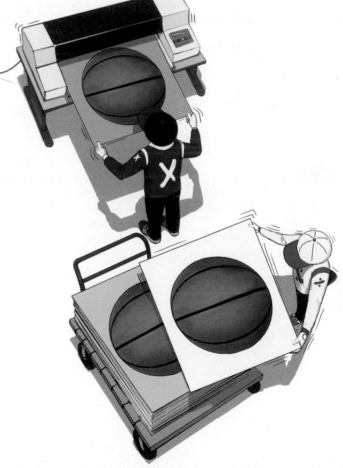

ISBN-13: 978-0-545-16074-2
ISBN-10: 0-545-16074-X

Text copyright © 2009 by Jerry Pallotta.
Illustrations copyright © 2009 by Rob Bolster.
All rights reserved. Published by Scholastic Inc.
SCHOLASTIC, Math = Fun!, and associated logos
are trademarks of Scholastic Inc.

12 11 10 9 8 7 6 5 4 3 2 1   9 10 11 12 13 14/0

Printed in the U.S.A.
First printing, September 2009

This is a multiplication sign. It is used to multiply numbers.

multiplication sign

Here is an equal sign. It is used to show that two or more numbers have the same value.

equal sign

We will use these pictures of different sports equipment to learn multiplication.

Pick up the baseball, basketball, soccer ball, football, or hockey puck.
Let the games begin! It is time to read about math.

2 x 2 = 4

An "equation" is a math sentence.
Two times two equals four is a multiplication equation.
Multiplication is a quick way to do addition.
OK, kick the soccer ball.

2 x 3 = 6

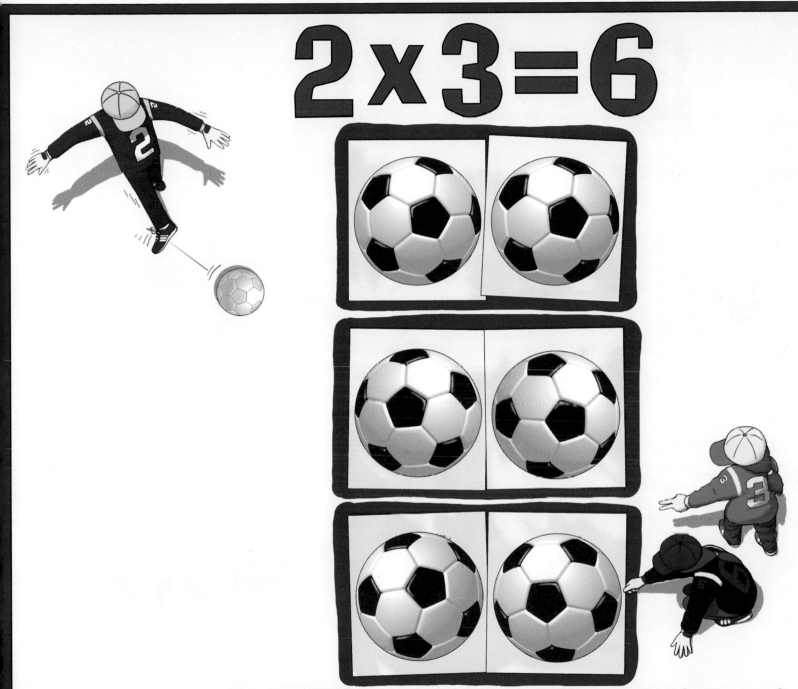

Nice kick! How many soccer balls are on this page?
One, two, three, four, five, six. Counting is one way to find the answer.
But there is an easier way to do this. Multiply!
Two times three equals six. See how fast that was?

2 x 4 = 8

Hike the football, then go out for a pass.
Each number in a multiplication equation has a name.
The numbers that are being multiplied are called "factors."
Two times four equals eight. On this page, the two and the four are factors.

2 x 5 = 10

Nice spiral. Great catch! Touchdown! When doing multiplication, the answer is called the "product." Two times five equals ten. The product is ten.
A factor times a factor equals the product.

3x2=6

Stop dribbling the basketball. Pay attention to the math. You have learned that two times three equals six. Three times two also equals six. The factors can be reversed and the product is still the same. Now throw a bounce pass.

3x3=9

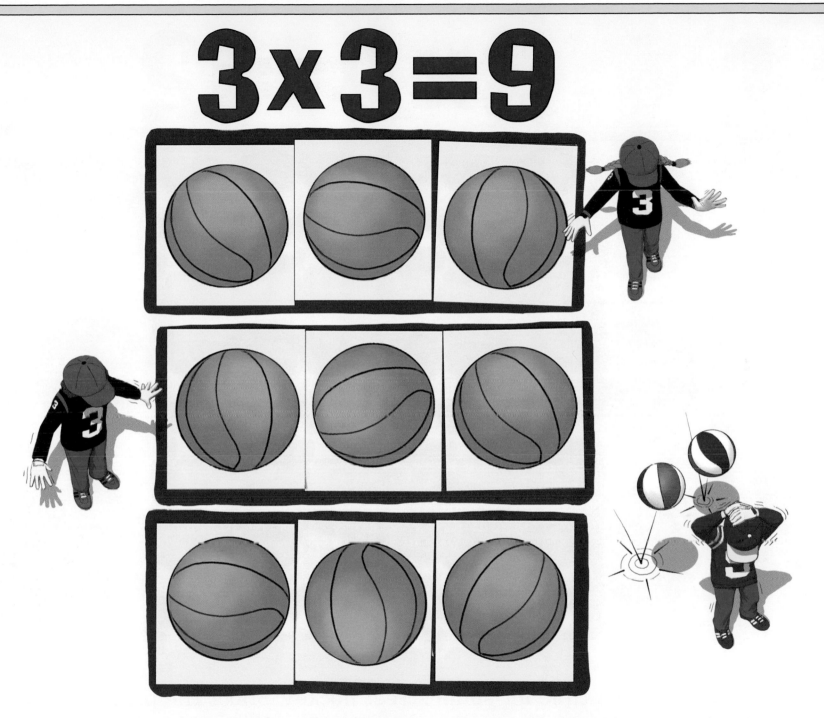

Bonk! Bonk! Not both at once! This equation is a slam dunk.
Three times three equals nine. When you multiply a number by itself,
the product is called a "square number."

3 x 4 = 12

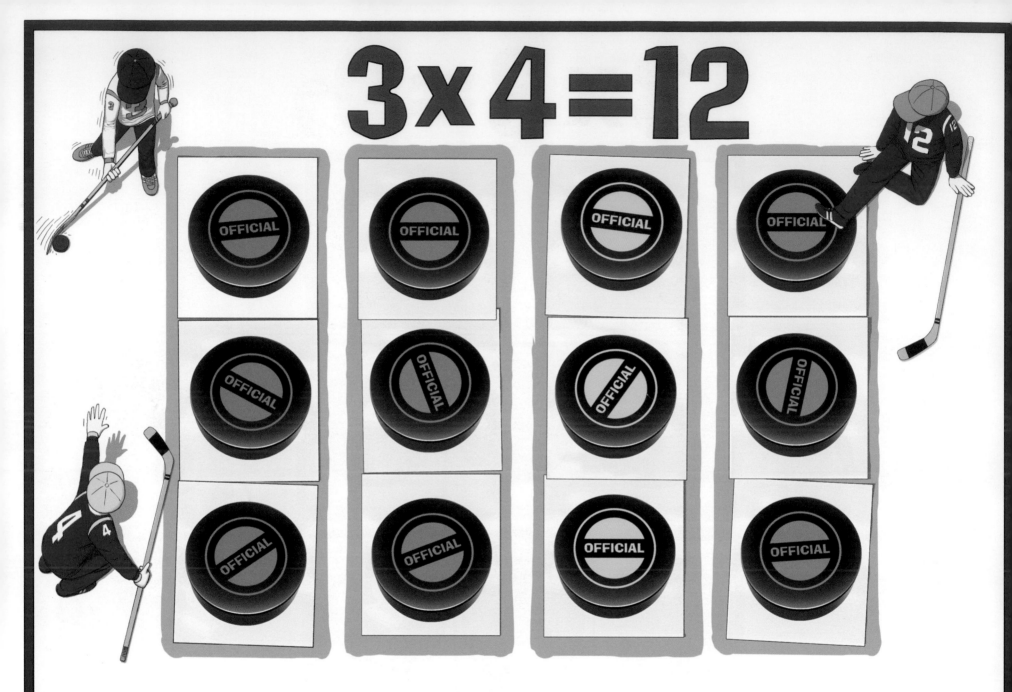

It's time for some street hockey. Shoot the puck.
Here are four groups of hockey pucks.
Each group is a different color. Count by threes: three, six, nine, twelve.
Three times four equals twelve.

3 x 5 = 15

Keep on multiplying! Three times five equals fifteen.
Score three goals: go for a hat trick!

$$\begin{array}{r} 4 \\ \times 4 \\ \hline 16 \end{array}$$

Let's play catch with the baseball. Multiplication equations can also be shown up and down—a vertical equation. Four times four equals sixteen. Sixteen is another square number. Remember, when a number is multiplied by itself, the product is a square number.

Nothing sounds as good as the crack of a bat.
Five times four equals twenty. Whoa! Twenty baseballs!
It's getting crowded in here.

Multiplication Tables

0×0=0					
1×0=0	1×1=1	1×2=2	1×3=3	1×4=4	1×5=5
2×0=0	2×1=2	2×2=4	2×3=6	2×4=8	2×5=10
3×0=0	3×1=3	3×2=6	3×3=9	3×4=12	3×5=15
4×0=0	4×1=4	4×2=8	4×3=12	4×4=16	4×5=20
5×0=0	5×1=5	5×2=10	5×3=15	5×4=20	5×5=25
6×0=0	6×1=6	6×2=12	6×3=18	6×4=24	6×5=30
7×0=0	7×1=7	7×2=14	7×3=21	7×4=28	7×5=35
8×0=0	8×1=8	8×2=16	8×3=24	8×4=32	8×5=40
9×0=0	9×1=9	9×2=18	9×3=27	9×4=36	9×5=45
10×0=0	10×1=10	10×2=20	10×3=30	10×4=40	10×5=50

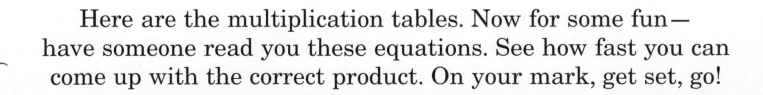

Here are the multiplication tables. Now for some fun—
have someone read you these equations. See how fast you can
come up with the correct product. On your mark, get set, go!

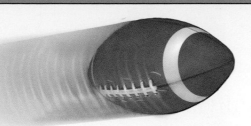

1x6=6	1x7=7	1x8=8	1x9=9	1x10=10
2x6=12	2x7=14	2x8=16	2x9=18	2x10=20
3x6=18	3x7=21	3x8=24	3x9=27	3x10=30
4x6=24	4x7=28	4x8=32	4x9=36	4x10=40
5x6=30	5x7=35	5x8=40	5x9=45	5x10=50
6x6=36	6x7=42	6x8=48	6x9=54	6x10=60
7x6=42	7x7=49	7x8=56	7x9=63	7x10=70
8x6=48	8x7=56	8x8=64	8x9=72	8x10=80
9x6=54	9x7=63	9x8=72	9x9=81	9x10=90
10x6=60	10x7=70	10x8=80	10x9=90	10x10=100

Can you identify the basketball, the baseball, the softball,
the hockey puck, the tennis ball, the golf ball, the volleyball, the football,
the soccer ball, the lacrosse ball, the field hockey ball, and the rugby ball?

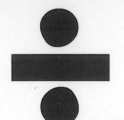

This is a division sign. It means "divided by."

division signs

This is also a division sign.
It also means "divided by," but people usually say "goes into."

Let's use sports equipment to learn division, too!

Take to the field and start dividing!

10÷2=5

Division is finding out how many times one number will go into another number. Don't be afraid. This isn't hardball. It's softball. Lob one in. Here is a division equation. Ten divided by two equals five. There are ten softballs. We divide by two. Each group has five in it.

$$4 \div 2 = 2$$

Swing your field hockey stick and flick a pass.
Four divided by two equals two. Each number in a division equation
has a name. The first number is called the "dividend."
Block the pass while dividing the field hockey balls.

6 ÷ 2 = 3

$$2\overline{)6}^{\,3}$$

Now wind up! Wham! Six divided by two equals three.
The second number in a division equation is called the "divisor."
You could say, two goes into six three times. The divisor is two.

8÷2=4

Eight divided by two equals four.
When dividing, the answer is called the "quotient."
What is the quotient in this equation? Ladies and gentlemen,
the quotient is four. Take a break and play some miniature golf.
The dividend divided by the divisor equals the quotient.

2x3=6

$$3 \overline{)6}^{\,2}$$

It's time for a putt. Keep your eye on the ball.
Multiplication and division are related. Six divided by three equals two.
Two times three equals six. Three times two equals six.

Pick up your lacrosse sticks and cradle the ball. Nine divided by three equals three. Remember, nine is a square number and three is the square root of nine. A square root sign is showed like this √ and is called a "radical." You would write the square root of nine equals three like this: √9 = 3.

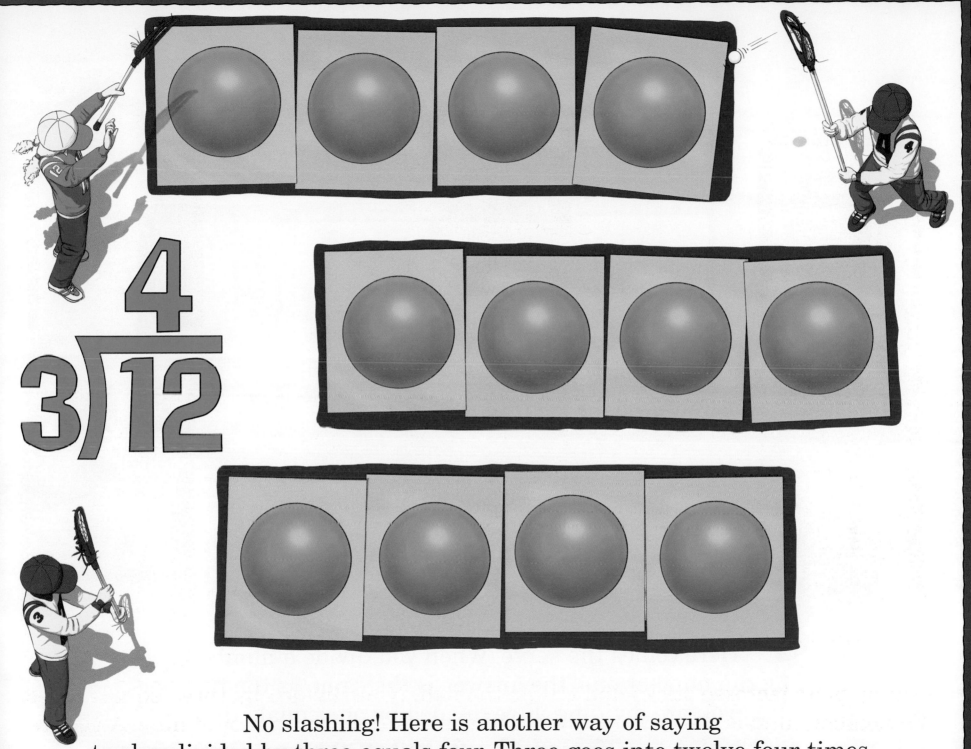

$$3\overline{)12} = 4$$

No slashing! Here is another way of saying
twelve divided by three equals four. Three goes into twelve four times.

5÷1=5

Here comes the serve. When you divide a number by the number one, the answer is the same as the number you are dividing. Five divided by one equals five.

54÷1=54   100÷1=100   3,000,000÷1=3,000,000

5 ÷ 5 = 1

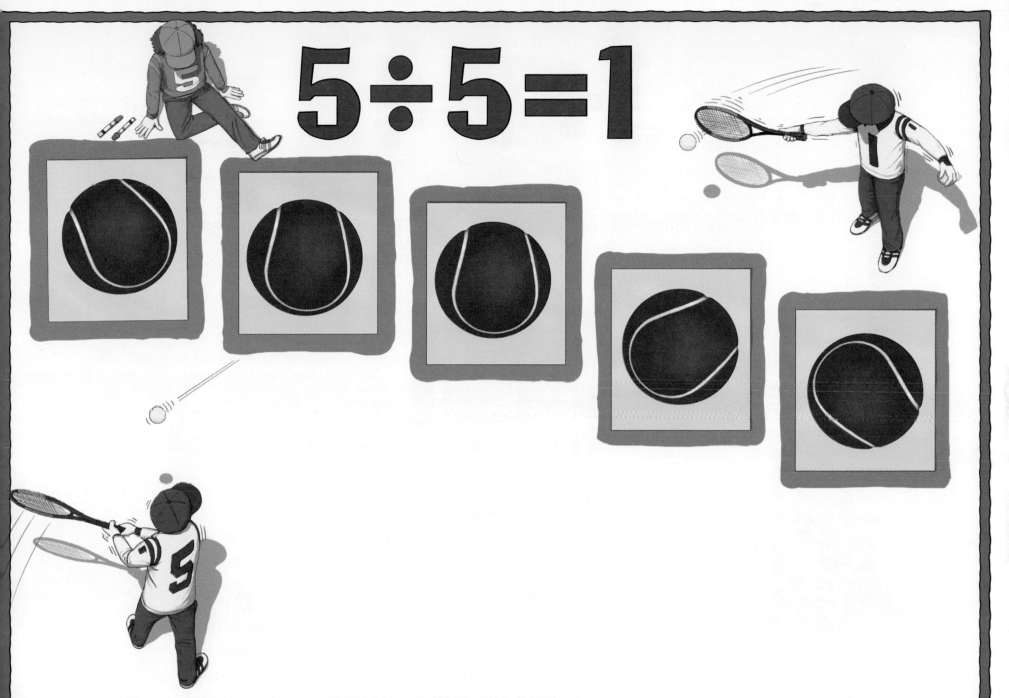

Match point!
Five divided by five equals one.
Whenever a number is divided by itself, the quotient is always one.

1÷1=1

Serve the volleyball over to your friend.
One divided by one equals one. Here is one colorful volleyball.
You will have more control hitting it back with two hands.

8÷4=2

Eight divided by four equals two. Unlike the factors in multiplication, in division, you cannot reverse the dividend and the divisor. Four divided by eight does not equal two.

Division Tables

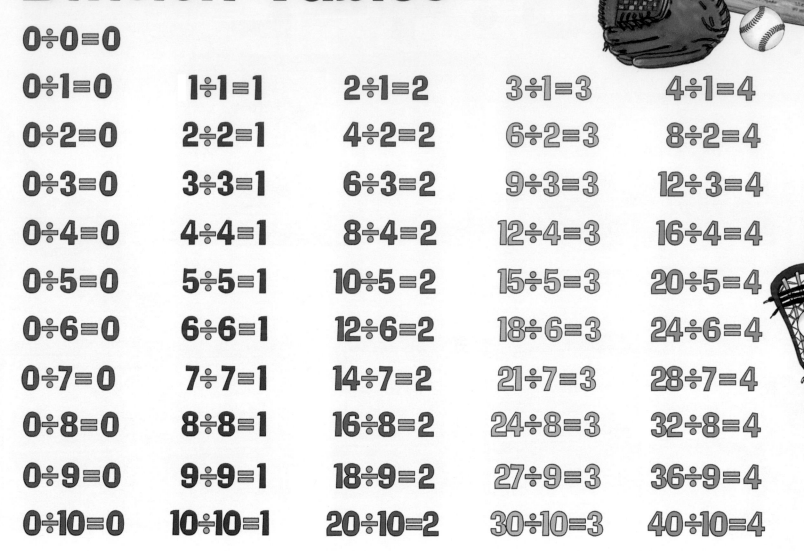

0÷0=0				
0÷1=0	1÷1=1	2÷1=2	3÷1=3	4÷1=4
0÷2=0	2÷2=1	4÷2=2	6÷2=3	8÷2=4
0÷3=0	3÷3=1	6÷3=2	9÷3=3	12÷3=4
0÷4=0	4÷4=1	8÷4=2	12÷4=3	16÷4=4
0÷5=0	5÷5=1	10÷5=2	15÷5=3	20÷5=4
0÷6=0	6÷6=1	12÷6=2	18÷6=3	24÷6=4
0÷7=0	7÷7=1	14÷7=2	21÷7=3	28÷7=4
0÷8=0	8÷8=1	16÷8=2	24÷8=3	32÷8=4
0÷9=0	9÷9=1	18÷9=2	27÷9=3	36÷9=4
0÷10=0	10÷10=1	20÷10=2	30÷10=3	40÷10=4

Memorize your division tables, too!
You will be using them for the rest of your life.

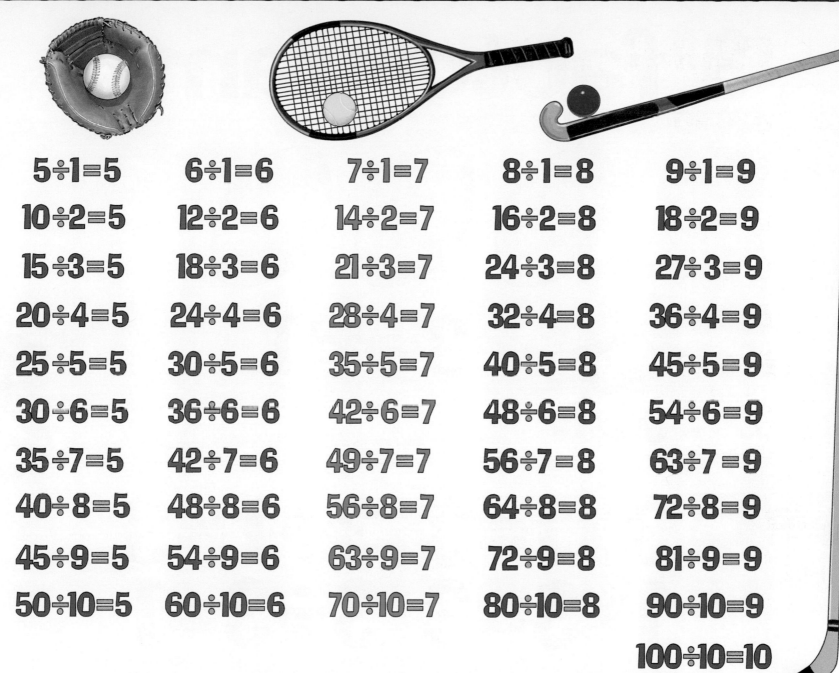

$$5 \div 1 = 5 \qquad 6 \div 1 = 6 \qquad 7 \div 1 = 7 \qquad 8 \div 1 = 8 \qquad 9 \div 1 = 9$$

$$10 \div 2 = 5 \qquad 12 \div 2 = 6 \qquad 14 \div 2 = 7 \qquad 16 \div 2 = 8 \qquad 18 \div 2 = 9$$

$$15 \div 3 = 5 \qquad 18 \div 3 = 6 \qquad 21 \div 3 = 7 \qquad 24 \div 3 = 8 \qquad 27 \div 3 = 9$$

$$20 \div 4 = 5 \qquad 24 \div 4 = 6 \qquad 28 \div 4 = 7 \qquad 32 \div 4 = 8 \qquad 36 \div 4 = 9$$

$$25 \div 5 = 5 \qquad 30 \div 5 = 6 \qquad 35 \div 5 = 7 \qquad 40 \div 5 = 8 \qquad 45 \div 5 = 9$$

$$30 \div 6 = 5 \qquad 36 \div 6 = 6 \qquad 42 \div 6 = 7 \qquad 48 \div 6 = 8 \qquad 54 \div 6 = 9$$

$$35 \div 7 = 5 \qquad 42 \div 7 = 6 \qquad 49 \div 7 = 7 \qquad 56 \div 7 = 8 \qquad 63 \div 7 = 9$$

$$40 \div 8 = 5 \qquad 48 \div 8 = 6 \qquad 56 \div 8 = 7 \qquad 64 \div 8 = 8 \qquad 72 \div 8 = 9$$

$$45 \div 9 = 5 \qquad 54 \div 9 = 6 \qquad 63 \div 9 = 7 \qquad 72 \div 9 = 8 \qquad 81 \div 9 = 9$$

$$50 \div 10 = 5 \qquad 60 \div 10 = 6 \qquad 70 \div 10 = 7 \qquad 80 \div 10 = 8 \qquad 90 \div 10 = 9$$

$$100 \div 10 = 10$$

And don't forget your gym bag. Put away the baseball bat, the glove, the catcher's mitt, the tennis racket, the field hockey stick, the ice hockey stick, the lacrosse stick, and the golf clubs.

3 factor family

3 and 1

$$3 \times 1 = 3 \qquad 3 \div 1 = 3$$
$$1 \times 3 = 3 \qquad 3 \div 3 = 1$$

"Factor families" show the relationship between multiplication and division equations. How many factors are in the factor family of the number three? Three and one are in the factor family of the number three. In case you are wondering, the kid is running with a rugby ball.

12 factor family
1, 2, 3, 4, 6, and 12

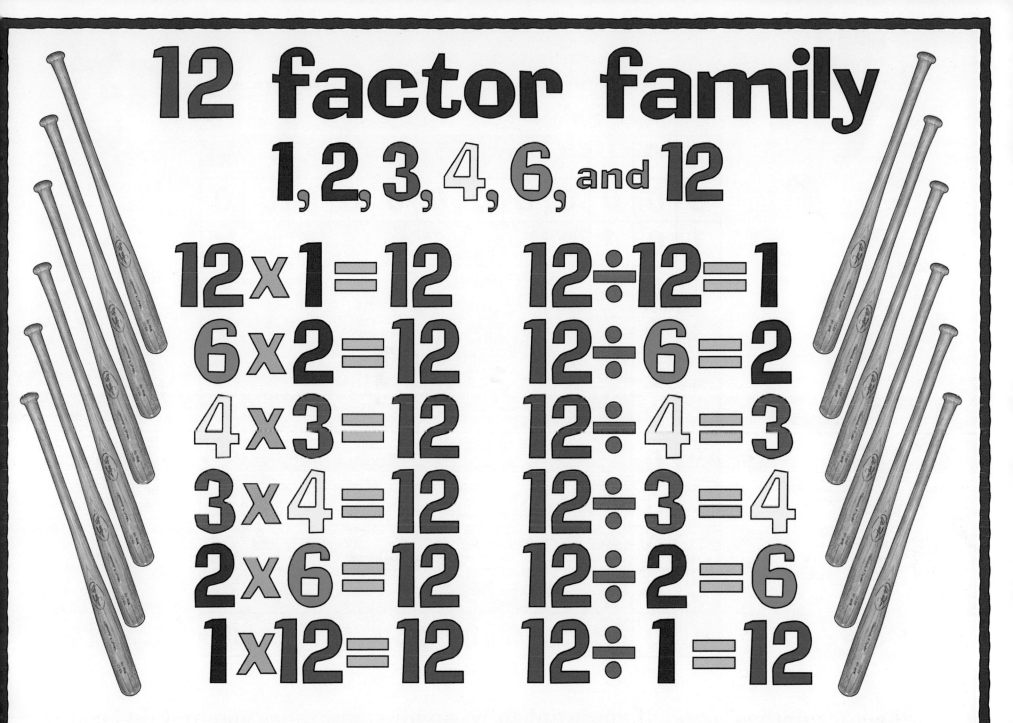

$12 \times 1 = 12$	$12 \div 12 = 1$
$6 \times 2 = 12$	$12 \div 6 = 2$
$4 \times 3 = 12$	$12 \div 4 = 3$
$3 \times 4 = 12$	$12 \div 3 = 4$
$2 \times 6 = 12$	$12 \div 2 = 6$
$1 \times 12 = 12$	$12 \div 1 = 12$

The numbers one, two, three, four, six, and twelve are in the factor family of the number twelve. Now pick up a bat, and hit a grand slam!

X	0	1	2	3	4	5	6	7	8	9	10
0	0	0	0	0	0	0	0	0	0	0	0
1	0	1	2	3	4	5	6	7	8	9	10
2	0	2	4	6	8	10	12	14	16	18	20
3	0	3	6	9	12	15	18	21	24	27	30
4	0	4	8	12	16	20	24	28	32	36	40
5	0	5	10	15	20	25	30	35	40	45	50
6	0	6	12	18	24	30	36	42	48	54	60
7	0	7	14	21	28	35	42	49	56	63	70
8	0	8	16	24	32	40	48	56	64	72	80
9	0	9	18	27	36	45	54	63	72	81	90
10	0	10	20	30	40	50	60	70	80	90	100

If you want to be an all-star,
review this mutiplication table.
We love sports, and we love to read about math!